AuthorHouse™ LLC
1663 Liberty Drive
Bloomington, IN 47403
www.authorhouse.com
Phone: 1-800-839-8640

© 2014 Frank DiPasquale. All rights reserved.

No part of this book may be reproduced, stored in a retrieval system, or transmitted by any means without the written permission of the author.

Published by AuthorHouse 08/23/2014

ISBN: 978-1-4969-3525-0 (sc)
978-1-4969-3526-7 (e)

Library of Congress Control Number: 2014915160

Any people depicted in stock imagery provided by Thinkstock are models, and such images are being used for illustrative purposes only.
Certain stock imagery © Thinkstock.

This book is printed on acid-free paper.

Because of the dynamic nature of the Internet, any web addresses or links contained in this book may have changed since publication and may no longer be valid. The views expressed in this work are solely those of the author and do not necessarily reflect the views of the publisher, and the publisher hereby disclaims any responsibility for them.

# Investing Conservatively in Retirement

## Make Your Money Work for You

Frank DiPasquale

Certified Financial Planner, CFP

I dedicate this book to my loving wife, Melissa. I don't know what I did right in my life to deserve her.

# Contents

Preface — vi

Introduction — vii

Chapter 1: Goal, Objectives, and Strategy — 1

Chapter 2: Setting Up the Asset Allocation — 3

Chapter 3: Setting Up the Criteria for Securities Chosen along with a Sample Portfolio — 5

Chapter 4: Determining the Withdrawal Rate — 10

Chapter 5: Performance of a Sample Portfolio — 11

Chapter 6: Monitoring the Portfolio and Rebalancing — 16

Chapter 7: Other Issues — 17

Chapter 8: Conclusion — 21

# Preface

During my time as a financial advisor it became very obvious that people needed guidance on how to manage their money in retirement. I found that, most of the time, books written with strategies for investing during retirement did not show examples of how to implement their strategies. When I tried to put these strategies into practice, they were either not practical or didn't accomplish the objective. I got fed up with reading fluff and decided to write this book to help everyday conservative people like me invest through retirement. This book was written for people that have worked hard to amass a lump sum of money, in the hope that it will allow them to lead a decent standard of living through retirement. This book discusses a conservative approach to investing, allowing you to build a portfolio that will generate a steady and increasing stream of income that should last thirty-plus years.

# Introduction

This book focuses on helping people maintain their standard of living in retirement by making their investments work for them, despite how the stock market is performing. You will be provided a strategy that will help to create a steady and increasing stream of income by setting up investments to generate a cash flow through dividends and interest.

This stream of income should supplement other income sources and keep pace with inflation. Other sources of income would typically include Social Security, pensions, rentals, etc. In order to maintain your lifestyle into retirement a recommended target of 80 to 100 percent of your preretirement income should be attained. This target should be adjusted by the following:

- Retirement savings is no longer a needed activity.
- Health costs typically increase as you get older so a cushion should be added.
- Health insurance costs can be another significant variable and will likely be from Medicare versus your pre-sixty-five insurance cost

Everyone's situation is different, so take a look at what costs will change in your retirement. The fact that you now have more free time on your hands in retirement, many times means that you spend more money. It would be a good idea to set up a retirement budget and monitor your spending to see what you are actually spending.

This book includes how stocks and mutual funds are selected and how to build and maintain a portfolio with this strategy. Also discussed is how and when to monitor and rebalance the portfolio. The sources of information needed to accomplish this strategy are identified along with the criteria used to select securities. This strategy selects securities that have proven track records that put the shareholder first, even through recessions like the recent great recession. This type of uninterrupted income stream should allow you the freedom from being at the whim of the day-to-day market volatility and let you sleep soundly at night.

After the recent great recession, many people are afraid of the stock market, and in a lot of cases, they just put their money into safe vehicles such as CDs, government bonds, money markets, or just savings accounts. If you have enough money to last you and/or your spouse for thirty years, without needing a higher than small growth rate, then this strategy is not for you, and you should stay in the federally guaranteed financial vehicles. However, if a low return may not be enough to keep you from running out of money, then you should seriously consider this strategy.

Some people that are still in the market are very fidgety and have concerns about the safety of their principal. However, they don't want to accept the slow growth of their money through CDs, savings accounts, government bonds, or other low-return vehicles. You can use financial advisors, but you need to pay them, which reduces your money. Also, dependent upon their competence or upon the strategy that they employ, your money may not have as high a probability of lasting the rest of your life. This book gives you the wherewithal to take control of your financial destiny.

If you follow this strategy, you should not be changing the securities very often. The exceptions would be if they are performing poorly or if there is a change in management, or because you are using a higher than recommended withdrawal rate. This book's method of investing should allow a layperson to set up his or her own portfolio, generate a cash flow, and still likely have money left over for heirs. A sample portfolio is constructed to show how to set up and execute this strategy.

Since higher-dividend stocks are less volatile than growth stocks, this strategy can also be used by people that are currently working but have a low risk tolerance. Over time, history has shown that growth stocks will outperform high-dividend stocks; however, in a down market and without a long time horizon, this may not be the case. If you cannot take the higher volatility of growth stocks, then you should seriously consider this strategy. If you are not retired and/or do not currently need the steady stream of income, you can have the dividends and interest redirected to buying more shares of securities, which will serve to accelerate the increase in your portfolio value.

Other issues discussed that would impact these investments and distributions include inflation, taxes, the Required Minimum Distribution (RMD), and unplanned life events.

# Chapter 1

## Goal, Objectives, and Strategy

*The Goal*

The goal is to have your portfolio generate an income stream that will supplement your other sources of income to help keep your standard of living through retirement.

*The Objectives*

The primary objective is to set up a portfolio that works for you by generating a steady and increasing stream of income that will last at least thirty years and keep up with inflation. The secondary objective is to grow your investments by the increasing value of these securities. An example of this strategy is shown in chapter 5 where the results after ten years show how a $500K portfolio became $845K even after $260K was withdrawn as an income stream over this period. These results show that the strategy's primary objective of generating a steady and increasing income stream and even the secondary objective of increasing the overall portfolio value were accomplished. As always, when you invest, past performance does not guarantee future results.

*The Strategy*

Regardless of the market's performance, the securities chosen in this portfolio must have proven track records of giving a steady and increasing stream of income averaging 4 percent of the original investment with an inflation adjustment. There are typically one to two recessions per decade, and during these time periods the last thing you want is to either receive reduced income from lower dividends/interest or maintain your income by selling securities. During a recession, securities are typically lowered in value, and the sale could jeopardize your portfolio value and your future cash flow. This is why a set of criteria was chosen to pick securities that do not have a history of reducing dividends during a recession. This fact along with a sufficient portfolio cash account should allow you to not have to sell securities to keep your steady stream of income during these time periods. The cash account receives in-flows from dividends/interest and distributes the cash to you on a regular basis.

Other advantages that a cash account gives include: it allows time to change securities, as necessary, in order to keep your portfolio strategy performing, and it acts as an emergency fund for unexpected events in life. Keep in mind that our primary objective is to maintain and establish a steady and increasing stream of income with capital appreciation being a secondary objective. You are buying securities mainly for the cash that they generate and not their appreciation performance. It is highly likely though, that a consistent cash-producing security also will have good price appreciation. If it does not have price appreciation when the stock market increases, then this could be a sign that something is going wrong with this security, and it should be reevaluated. The stocks that are selected should show a track record of not only holding a steady stream of dividends but also increasing them. There are no guarantees when investing, but you can certainly reduce the risk with a steady stream of income.

The fixed investments chosen in this strategy are short-term bonds and floating-rate bank loans that will typically fluctuate with inflation, so if the economy is in an inflationary period, the interest cash flow will go up. If the economy is in a decreasing interest period, then the fixed investments will have decreased cash flows. These types of securities were chosen to minimize the effects of inflation. Inflation is discussed in a later section.

The real estate fund criteria for this strategy invests in REITs and real estate related activities, which adds diversity, a higher cash flow, professional management, and the same priority of objectives as this book's strategy. Over the past ten years, the cash outflow of the selected real estate fund, for the sample portfolio, ranged from 3.9 to 8.1 percent of the original investment.

# Chapter 2

## Setting Up the Asset Allocation

The first step for building a portfolio is to set-up the asset allocation. The asset allocation will be diversified with securities chosen so that a substantial amount of the withdrawal will be covered by dividends and interest. Based on the withdrawal chart in chapter 5, if the withdrawal rate is 4 percent of the original portfolio value plus an inflation adjustment, then the portfolio is projected to last thirty-plus years. An advantage of this withdrawal rate with this strategy is that you should not be forced to sell your securities at an inopportune time. In order to have this money available, we have the cash account set up as a flow-through and buffer for the portfolio. The asset allocation should be set up as follows:

| | | |
|---|---|---|
| Cash | 20% | |
| Equity | 50% | stocks |
| Fixed | 20% | bond fund, floating rate bank loan fund |
| Real Estate | 10% | real estate fund |

The stocks should show a track record over the past ten years of steady and increasing dividends, regardless of how the economy or the company is doing. The timeframe of ten years was chosen because it is long enough to show a trend in the fluctuating domestic and global economy. The increasing dividend requirement is what is needed to keep up with the devaluation of the dollar over time (inflation).

Stocks are a major part of this asset allocation because they also have more opportunity to appreciate in value and therefore boost the value of your portfolio while they are generating a cash flow that you are using. A sample portfolio with the recommended withdrawal rate, corresponding cash flow, and appreciation over a ten-year period is shown in chapter 5.

The fixed asset class is represented by short-term bonds and floating-rate bank loans. Mutual funds were used for this class because a higher return than the going rate is needed. In order to get that higher return, we need to take more risk. Using mutual funds reduces risk by giving diversity, more securities to dilute the poor performance of a specific security, and professional management. The advantage of these fixed vehicles is that the cash flow should mimic inflation, thereby minimizing the effect of increasing or decreasing interest rates in the economy. The disadvantage of these vehicles is that capital appreciation is likely to be minimal. This topic is discussed further in chapter 7.

The real estate fund invests in real estate through equity and debt REITs, as well as other real estate activities throughout the world. The professional management, diversity, and high cash flow are key attributes to investing in this sector. Professional management and diversity lets this fund take on more risk, which allows for a higher cash flow.

Since the cash account is 20 percent of the portfolio, the securities will be 80 percent, which means that they currently need to generate an overall return of 5+ percent to enable a cash outflow of

4 percent plus inflation adjustments. Given that the strategy is targeting a dividend/interest cash flow of 4 percent plus an inflation adjustment, and 5+ percent is needed from the securities, then the extra 1+ percent will need to come from dividend growth and/or the sale of securities. Over the long term, stocks typically have an annual growth rate of 10+ percent and bonds 5 to 8 percent, so if only 1+ percent is needed from dividend growth and/or the sale of securities, this should not reduce the value of your original portfolio but allow it to grow. Of course, with increasing dividends and a cash account buffer you may find that you do not have to sell securities for a very long time. Refer to chapter 5 for an example of how this strategy has performed over the past ten years on a sample portfolio.

All dividends and interest should go to the cash account and not be reinvested. Withdrawals will come out of the cash account to allow for the original investments to increase or decrease in value without impacting the withdrawal rate of the original portfolio.

We are targeting a stream of income that gives the greater of 4 percent of the original investment plus inflation or the RMD. The 20 percent cash account is a cushion, which allows for recessions, stock market volatility, unplanned withdrawals due to unexpected events with the economy or your personal situation. This cushion should last several years before you would need to sell securities to replenish the account. If the securities are performing as planned, they will be generating a cash in-flow to accommodate your withdrawals, while you wait for the market to recover, further delaying any sale of securities.

# Chapter 3

## Setting Up the Criteria for Securities Chosen along with a Sample Portfolio

The criteria were established to find companies or funds that have generated a stream of income for shareholders despite the state of the domestic or global economies. Past performance is no guarantee of future results; however, the past does give you a good look at a security's success and the success of management.

Due to the thousands of securities to choose from, it is necessary to use screeners to find the securities that meet this strategy's requirements. The criteria and screeners used to find securities include the following;

**Criteria**

a. Equities as Stocks. Stock screeners that were used included; www.finviz.com, www.morningstar.com, and www.fidelity.com.

   i. Market cap of +$2B.

   ii. A dividend that is at least 3.5% of the stock price.

   iii. A 5 year **average** past dividend growth of at least 3.0% per year

   iv. A 5 year **average** earnings per share (eps) of past growth should be at least 3.0% per year.

   v. A dividend that has stayed the same or increased each year, over the last 10 years.

   vi. The dividend payout ratio should typically be less than 70% but may be higher dependent upon the industry. You can find peer companies' data on websites such as www.morningstar.com.

   vii. Debt/equity ratio should typically be less than 70% but here again is dependent upon the industry. You can find peer companies' data on websites such as www.morningstar.com.

   viii. A CEO who has been in place for at least 5 years.

b. Fixed Investments: Short-Term Bonds and Floating Bank Loans

   At this time, in order to get the higher interest needed for this strategy, the risk taken is higher, and therefore mutual funds were chosen instead of specific entity securities. The funds will spread out the risk and take advantage of professional management. Fund screeners used included www.morningstar.com and www.fidelity.com.

    i. Market cap of +$2B

    ii. Yields over 3.0% consistently

    iii. A duration less than 2.5 years

    iv. Fund manager who has a minimum of 5 years with the fund

    v. A risk rating of B or better

c. Real Estate: Real Estate Fund

In order to get a higher dividend, the risk taken is higher, and therefore mutual funds were used instead of specific entity securities. The fund will spread out the risk and take advantage of professional management. The real estate sector also gives added diversity to the portfolio. Fund screeners used included; www.morningstar.com and www.fidelity.com.

    i. Objectives that are in line with this book's strategy

    ii. Market cap of +$2B

    iii. Yields over 3.0% consistently

    iv. Fund manager who has a minimum of 5 years with the fund

    v. A low risk rating

    vi. Diversity in the sector

Reasoning for each of the criteria is as follows:

**Stocks**:

    i. Market cap +$2B—size gives stability for a misstep by a company to allow it to recover.

    ii. Dividend that is at least 3.5% of original stock price—this number will change for stocks as the price goes up and down, but the absolute value should stay the same or increase from year to year.

    iii. A 5 year average past dividend growth of at least 3.0% per year—a dividend may not grow every year, but growth over time means that management is clearly looking out for their shareholders and not just stockpiling the money.

iv. A 5 year average earnings per share (eps) of past growth should be at least 3.0% per year—since the dividends come out of the eps, you need long-term growth from the eps to have the opportunity to have long-term dividend growth.

v. A dividend that has stayed the same or increased each year, over the last 10 years—the dividend trend shows a consistency of how the company is managed and the regard for shareholders.

vi. The dividend payout should typically be less than 70% but may be higher dependent upon the industry—companies use the eps for several uses, including: to give out dividends, invest in projects to grow their company, acquire other companies, build an emergency fund for recessionary periods, etc. This is why most companies keep their payout ratio of dividends to eps low enough to allow for these other activities. Companies that typically use a higher than 70% payout ratio have a more stable cash flow, such as telecom or utility companies. Peer companies' data should be reviewed and can be found on www.morningstar.com.

vii. Debt/equity ratio should typically be less than 70%, but here again this is dependent upon the industry – the debt/equity ratio is a good indicator of the financial soundness of a company. The higher the ratio, the more unstable a company is. Here again, the consistency of cash flow and the capital intensiveness of an industry could push companies to use higher ratios. Check the peer companies' ratios on www.morningstar.com.

viii. A CEO who has been in place for at least 5 years—the CEO steers the ship, so if the leader changes, there is a risk involved with future performance of the company.

**Fixed:**

i. Market cap of +$2B. Size gives stability for a misstep by a fund to allow it to recover.

ii. Yields over 3.0% consistently. Interest income should increase and decrease with inflation.

iii. A duration that is less than 2.5 years. The short duration allows the fund to keep current with interest rates whether they increase or decrease.

iv. Fund manager who has a minimum of 5 years with the fund. The fund manager typically executes a consistent strategy.

v. A risk rating of B or better. In order to get interest income at higher than the going rate, we have to take a higher risk. Having a mutual fund allows the diversity to withstand some poor performances of specific securities in the fund. Professional management should allow for enhanced performance of a higher-risk fund.

**Real Estate:**

i. Objectives that are in line with this book's strategy. The fund chosen should have a primary objective of a high cash flow and capital appreciation as a secondary objective.

ii. Market cap of +$2B. This size gives stability for a misstep by a fund to allow it to recover.

iii. Yields over 3.0% consistently. Risk, diversity, and professional management within this sector should allow for higher dividend yields.

iv. A fund manager who has a minimum of 5 years with the fund. Typically, if successful, a fund manager will execute a consistent strategy.

v. A low risk rating. Diversity and professional management should allow this fund to perform. The risk rating can be found on www.morningstar.com.

vi. Diversity in the sector. The mutual fund should have diversity and professional management to help with the consistency of this cash flow. Diversity can be accomplished with different types of real estate equities, debt, and other related activities.

If you are having a problem filling your portfolio with stocks that meet all of the criteria, then you can make an exception for one of the criterion other than the criterion that shows that management puts the shareholder first. This criterion would be that the company has not reduced the dividend regardless of the economy and/or company results.

When choosing securities for your portfolio, it is important to pay attention to the loads and fees charged. It is very likely that you can find no-load and lower expense fee securities that perform just as well as securities with loads and higher expense fees. In some instances this is not the case, and then you have to decide if the added performance is worth the loading and/or higher expenses. Sometimes your discount broker (Fidelity, Charles Schwab, TD Ameritrade, etc.) has a load-waiving agreement for certain securities, so check with them when investigating a security.

In order to validate this strategy, a sample portfolio of $500K was made up of ten stocks, three funds, and a cash account shown in the charts below. The result for this portfolio over the past ten years (2004–2013) was;

- a distribution of $260K
- a cash account balance that started at $100K and became $58K
- a total portfolio value that started at $500K and became $845K
- no securities needed to be sold to accommodate the $260K of withdrawals over the 10 years

Details of the performance for this portfolio are shown and discussed in chapter 5.

## Equities

| Stocks | div yld,% | 5yr div grth,% | 5yr eps grth,% | Payout ratio,% | debt/equity ratio | yrs of not reducing div | Sector |
|---|---|---|---|---|---|---|---|
| COP | 4.2 | 7.5 | 21 | 36 | 0.42 | 10 | Oil & gas |
| POT | 4.2 | 43 | 17 | 52 | 0.36 | 10 | Agriculture |
| BNS | 4.1 | 8.6 | 11 | 47 | 0.16 | 10 | Financial |
| TD | 3.6 | 6.6 | 6.9 | 46 | 0.21 | 10 | Financial |
| MCD | 3.4 | 10 | 8.1 | 56 | 0.89 | 10 | Restaurant |
| INTC | 3.6 | 6.8 | 16 | 47 | 0.23 | 10 | Technology |
| DGAS | 3.7 | 2.5 | 5.2 | 68 | 0.77 | 10 | Utilities |
| ED | 4.4 | 4.2 | 2.2 | 69 | 1 | 25 | Utilities |
| PNW | 4.1 | 1 | 7.2 | 45 | 0.83 | 10 | Electricity & *RE |
| SCG | 4.2 | 4.4 | 2.8 | 44 | 1.27 | 10 | Elec & gas |

Data is from 12/31/2013

## Fixed Income and Real Estate Securities

| | Duration, years | Manager tenure | Dividend, % | Dividend track record, years | Market cap, $B | Credit rating |
|---|---|---|---|---|---|---|
| LALDX | 2.1 | 16 | 3.7 | 10 | 35 | BB |
| EAFAX | 0.2 | 17 | 4.4 | 10 | 7.7 | B |
| FRIFX | N/A | 11 | 3.9 | 10 | 3.8 | Low |

Data is from 12/31/2013

*Real Estate

# Chapter 4

## Determining the Withdrawal Rate

The withdrawal rate is critical in determining how long your money will last. It is recommended that you withdraw the greater of the Required Minimum Distribution (RMD) or 4 percent of the original portfolio amount, adjusted for inflation every year. If a 4 percent withdrawal rate of your original portfolio, adjusted for inflation, is not enough when combined with your other income sources, you would need to either increase the withdrawal rate or reduce your standard of living. Keep in mind that increasing the withdrawal rate may jeopardize your money from lasting thirty-plus years. The different withdrawal rates and the projected impact on the longevity of your money are shown in the upcoming chart.

The RMD is a government mandate that requires people that reach the age of 70½ to withdraw a certain percentage of their money that has not been taxed (pretax accounts such as IRA, 401(k), 457, etc.). A higher RMD withdrawal rate than the recommended 4 percent of the original investment plus inflation withdrawal rate is a good problem to have, since it means that your investments are growing nicely.

The chart below shows the length of time that money is projected to last at different inflation adjusted withdrawal rates for a $500k portfolio. The breakdown of this hypothetical portfolio is similar to the asset allocation in this book's recommendation.

**Withdrawal Rates**

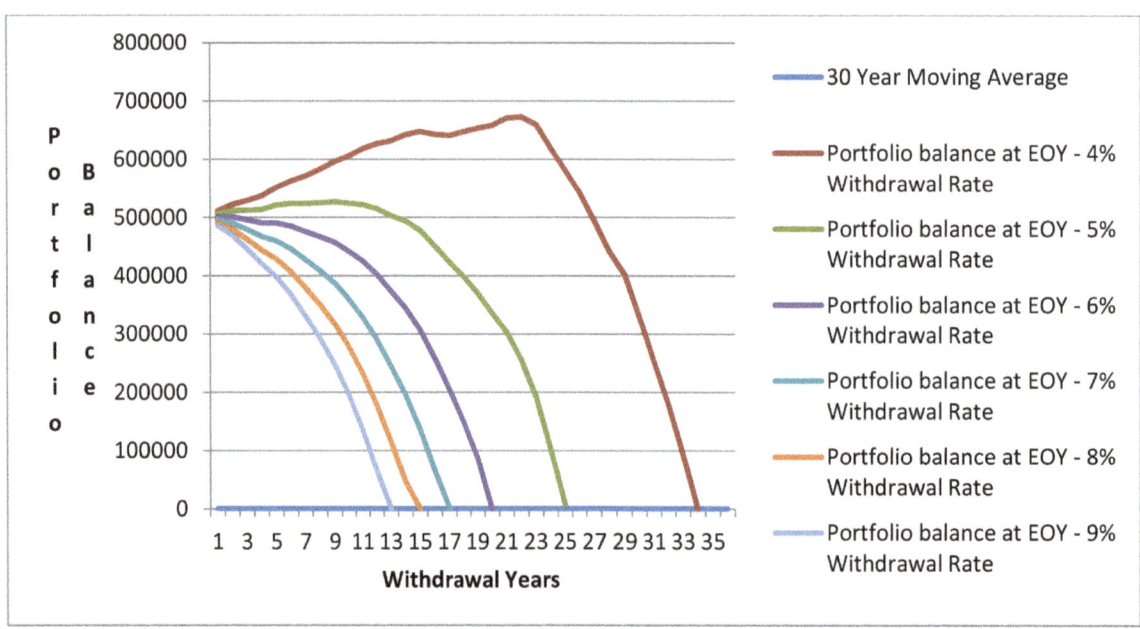

The chart is based on a 30 year moving average that runs through the years of 1950-1980 with data that spans 1950-2013. The hypothetical portfolio is made up of 50% equities (S&P 500 index), 30% bonds (10 year treasuries) and 20% of short term investments (3 month treasuries).

# Chapter 5

## Performance of a Sample Portfolio

The primary purpose of this strategy is to get a steady and increasing cash flow that keeps up with inflation and allows your money to last at least thirty years. The secondary goal is to have appreciation of your portfolio.

If you had the portfolio mentioned in chapter 3 from 12/31/03 to 12/31/13, the results are shown below. These results include an annual withdrawal of the greater of the RMD or 4 percent of the original portfolio, adjusted for inflation.

|  | Initial Investment | | | | Investment after 10 years | | | | |
|---|---|---|---|---|---|---|---|---|---|
|  | 2003 div yld based on the 12/31/03 stk price, % | 12/31/2003 stock price $ | 12/31/03 shares purchased | 12/31/03 initial portfolio value $ | 2013 div yld based on the 12/31/03 stk price, % | 2013 div yld based on the 12/31/13 stk price, % | 12/31/13 stk price $ |  | **12/31/13 portfolio value $** |
| Stocks | | | | | | | | | |
| COP | 3.5 | 25.17 | 993 | 25000 | 10.5 | 4.2 | 70.65 | | 70155 |
| POT | 1.2 | 4.82 | 5187 | 25000 | 24.6 | 4.2 | 32.96 | | 170964 |
| BNS | 4.3 | 25.45 | 982 | 25000 | 9.3 | 4.1 | 62.55 | | 61424 |
| TD | 3.8 | 16.71 | 1496 | 25000 | 9.4 | 3.6 | 47.12 | | 70492 |
| MCD | 2.2 | 24.83 | 1007 | 25000 | 12.5 | 3.4 | 97.03 | | 97709 |
| INTC | 0.5 | 32.05 | 780 | 25000 | 2.7 | 3.6 | 25.96 | | 20249 |
| DGAS | 4.9 | 11.98 | 2087 | 25000 | 6 | 3.7 | 22.38 | | 46707 |
| ED | 5.3 | 43.01 | 581 | 25000 | 5.8 | 4.4 | 55.28 | | 32118 |
| PNW | 4.5 | 40.02 | 625 | 25000 | 5.5 | 4.1 | 52.92 | | 33075 |
| SCG | 4.2 | 34.25 | 730 | 25000 | 5.9 | 4.2 | 46.93 | | 34259 |
|  |  |  | Sub | 250000 |  |  |  | Sub | 637,152 |
| Fixed | | | | | | | | | |
| LALDX | 2.4 | 4.49 | 11136 | 50000 | 3.2 | 3.7 | 4.55 | | 50669 |
| EAFAX | 3.1 | 11.27 | 4437 | 50000 | 5.6 | 4.4 | 11.06 | | 49073 |
|  |  |  | Sub | 100000 |  |  |  | Sub | 99,742 |
| Real Estate | | | | | | | | | |
| FRIFX | 6.9 | 11.3 | 4425 | 50000 | 6.9 | 3.9 | 11.32 | | 50091 |
|  |  |  | Sub | 50000 |  |  |  | Sub | 50091 |
|  |  |  |  |  |  | **cash withdrawn** | 260608 | | |
|  |  |  |  |  |  | **cash generated** | 218150 | | |
| Cash |  |  | Sub | 100000 |  |  |  | Sub | 57542 |
|  |  | **Portfolio Value** |  | 500000 |  |  |  |  | 844527 |

As the sample portfolio shows, there was no sale of securities and all of the cash flow that was generated and withdrawn was done through the cash account. Over the ten-year period, $260K was withdrawn as income; the cash account reduced from $100K to $58K and the overall portfolio value increased from $500K to $845K.

In order to evaluate the capital appreciation of the securities in this strategy, a comparison is shown below for the ten-year performance of stocks and fixed securities versus their benchmarks. The S&P 500 index was used for stocks and the Barclay's U.S. Capital Aggregate Index for the fixed securities.

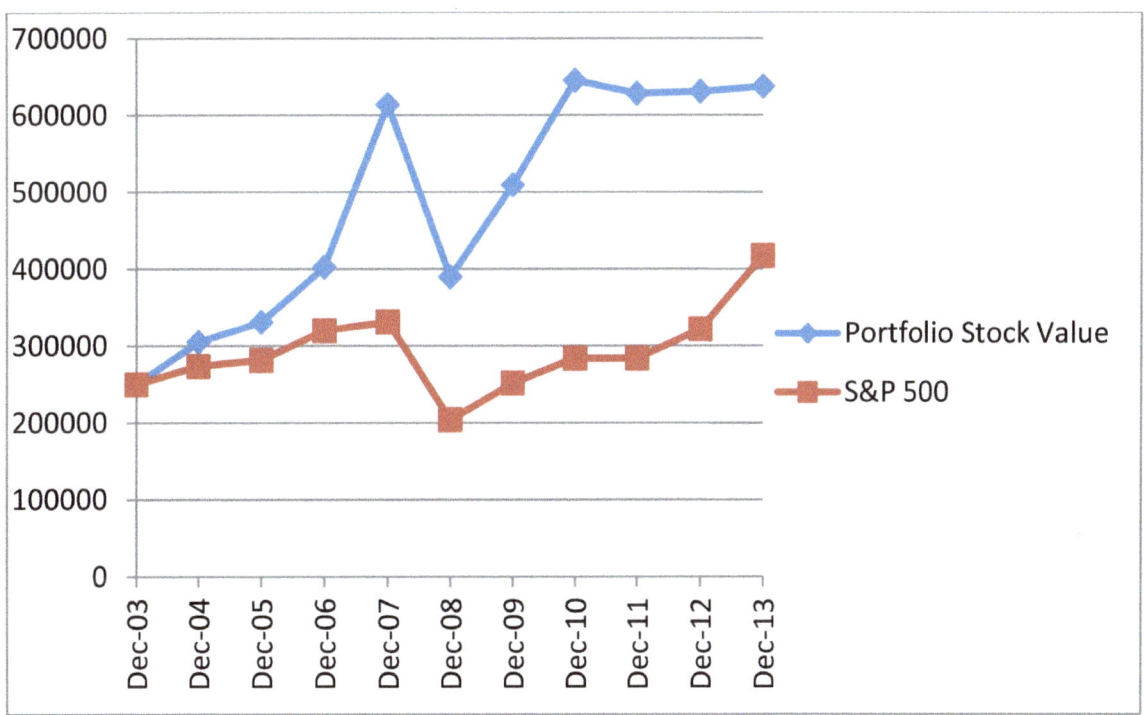

As can be seen on the above chart, over this ten-year period the capital appreciation for these high-dividend stocks substantially outperformed the S&P 500 index. This outperformance occurred while these stocks were an integral part in generating a cash flow of $260K over this time period.

**Portfolio Fixed Securities (LALDX AND EAFAX) vs Barclay's U.S. Capital Aggregate Index**

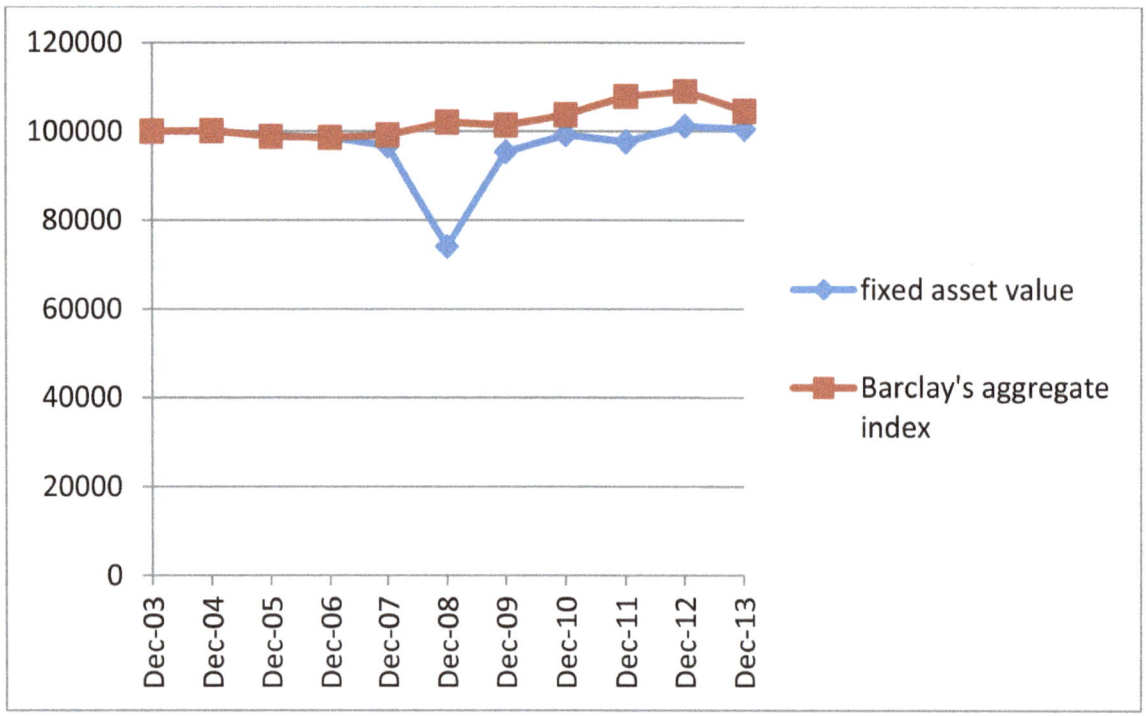

In the above chart the portfolio's fixed investments show more volatility than the Barclay index but the principal amount essentially remains the same while generating a portion of the $260K cash flow over this ten-year period.

The next two charts show the cash account activity and the separate account balances along with the total portfolio value over the ten-year period.

## Cash account activity over the ten-year period

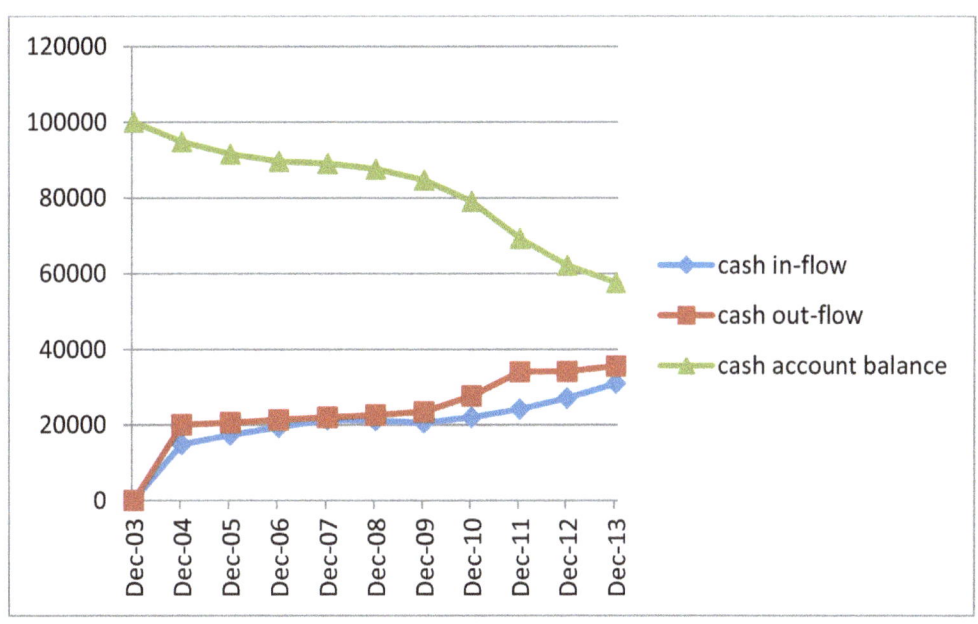

## Total portfolio value change from 12/31/2003 to 12/31/2013 plus the four asset classes that make it up

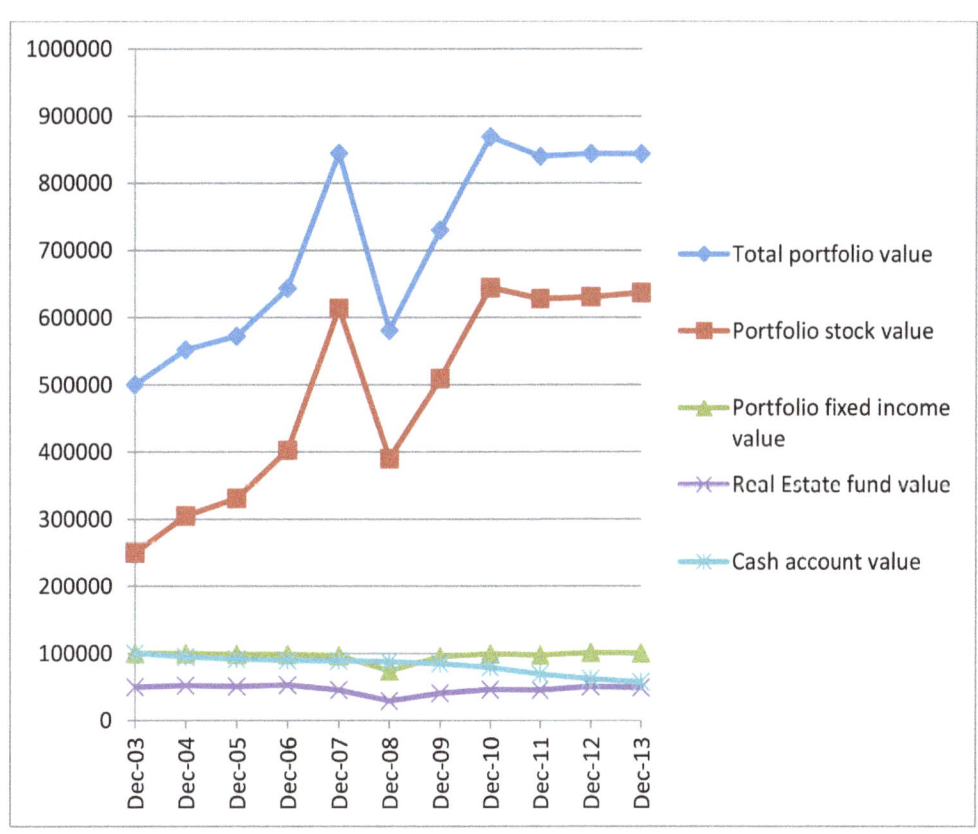

*The charts above show that, despite the withdrawal of $260K over the ten-year period, this strategy not only accomplished the first goal of generating steady and increasing cash flow but also increased in value at the same time.* Keep in mind that when you invest, past performance does not guarantee future results.

# Chapter 6

## Monitoring the Portfolio and Rebalancing

Stability of your cash flow:

In order to maintain your cash flow you need to be aware of any significant events that occur with your investments. Will it jeopardize your cash flow? If you are not sure or don't know, then replace the security. Examples of significant events would be:

- An oil spill by BP in the Gulf of Mexico
- Change in leadership of a company or mutual fund
- A change in direction by current management
- A technology change or breakthrough

The investments should be reviewed once a year or when you find out that a significant event has taken place. You should make sure that the securities still meet the criteria and that the cash flow is not at risk due to a substantial change.

The macro economy will have an impact on securities. If interest rates rise significantly, then you should take a look at your fixed securities. The returns on the floating-rate fund (EAFAX) and short-term bond fund (LALDX) should keep up with the changing interest rates. However, you can take advantage of high interest rates by locking into the high rates with long-term bonds, which will increase your cash flow and appreciate your portfolio as interest rates go down. If you are uncomfortable making this type of change, then either consult a financial professional or leave your portfolio alone since the cash flow with your current fixed securities should keep pace with inflation.

The *withdrawal rate* should be reviewed if something changes in your life where you need a higher cash flow. If you need a lump sum and have to sell securities, then you should reevaluate your withdrawal rate as to how it will affect your lifestyle and determine how long your investment is projected to last (refer to the withdrawal rate chart in chapter 4). Also, once you are 70½ or older, each year, you should calculate both your RMD and 4 percent of the original portfolio plus inflation, so you can determine your withdrawal amount, which should be the larger of the two calculations.

*Rebalancing* should not occur very often since there is a lot of cushion with this cash flow strategy. Rebalancing the portfolio should be similar to a reset of the original asset allocation. The portfolio should be rebalanced when the cash account balance dips below 50 percent of its original balance. At this point, you would cash in your poorest-performing stock(s) so that the cash account balance is 20 percent and buy/sell your fixed and real estate funds so they are back to the 10 percent share each of the total *current* portfolio.

# Chapter 7

## Other Issues

Issues discussed here include: the Required Minimum Distribution (RMD), inflation, and taxes.

### *Required Minimum Distribution (RMD)*

The government wants its taxes, so they require minimum withdrawals on tax-deferred accounts such as 401(k), IRA, 457, and other pretax accounts when you turn 70½. If the withdrawal from the plan(s) does not meet the minimum requirement, there will be a 50 percent tax on the shortfall amount. The RMD rate is calculated by dividing the portfolio's total balance, from the end of the most recent prior year, by the distribution period shown on the table below, next to your age.

For example, let's say you turn 75½ this year (2014). Since the table below is current, then you would take your balance at the end of 2013 and divide by the distribution number from the table. If your balance is $600,000 at the end of 2013, then you would divide this by 22.9 (from the table) and your RMD would be $26,201. Note that this is 4.37% of your total portfolio balance as of the end of the prior year. You should also calculate the 4% plus the cumulative inflation rate of the original portfolio. This would be calculated by taking the original portfolio value and multiplying it by the 4% plus the cumulative inflation rate or $500,000 x 5.64% and would be $28,200. Since the $28,200 is higher, it would be withdrawn to maintain your current lifestyle. The cumulative inflation rate is also shown on the table.

Table

The table below shows the *Required Minimum Distribution (RMD)* rate versus the recommended withdrawal rate of 4 percent of the original portfolio, increased by a typical inflation rate of 3.5 percent each year. Withdrawals start at sixty-five years of age and are shown until one hundred.

This table is for owners of the deferred accounts who are single or whose spouses are not ten years or more younger. If spouses are more than ten years younger, then the applicable table would be found in publication 590 on the www.irs.gov website. Publication 590 should be used every year to do the RMD calculations since they have the updated tables. Actual inflation rates should also be used in your calculations. These rates can be found on this same government website and are discussed below.

Note that in the calculations, the portfolio value used for the RMD calculation *(end of most recent prior year)* differs from the portfolio value (original value) used with 4 percent plus inflation of the *original* portfolio value. Once you are 70½ you should calculate the RMD annually to determine what withdrawal amount is necessary to avoid the 50 percent tax penalty. You should also calculate the 4 percent plus inflation number and withdraw the higher of the two calculations for your cash flow. If you are uncomfortable calculating your RMD each year, then speak to the IRS or your financial advisor.

| Required Minimum Distribution for owners who are single or whose spouses are not 10 years or more younger ||||
|---|---|---|---|
| Age | distribution period | necessary RMD w/d rate | 4% initial w/d rate plus a 3.5% annual cumulative inflation increase |
| 65 |  | 0 | 4 |
| 66 |  | 0 | 4.14 |
| 67 |  | 0 | 4.28 |
| 68 |  | 0 | 4.43 |
| 69 |  | 0 | 4.59 |
| 70 | 27.4 | 3.65 | 4.75 |
| 71 | 26.5 | 3.77 | 4.92 |
| 72 | 25.6 | 3.91 | 5.09 |
| 73 | 24.7 | 4.05 | 5.27 |
| 74 | 23.8 | 4.20 | 5.45 |
| 75 | 22.9 | 4.37 | 5.64 |
| 76 | 22 | 4.55 | 5.84 |
| 77 | 21.2 | 4.72 | 6.04 |
| 78 | 20.3 | 4.93 | 6.26 |
| 79 | 19.5 | 5.13 | 6.47 |
| 80 | 18.7 | 5.35 | 6.70 |
| 81 | 17.9 | 5.59 | 6.94 |
| 82 | 17.1 | 5.85 | 7.18 |
| 83 | 16.3 | 6.13 | 7.43 |
| 84 | 15.5 | 6.45 | 7.69 |
| 85 | 14.8 | 6.76 | 7.96 |

| 86 | 14.1 | 7.09 | 8.24 |
|---|---|---|---|
| 87 | 13.4 | 7.46 | 8.53 |
| 88 | 12.7 | 7.87 | 8.82 |
| 89 | 12 | 8.33 | 9.13 |
| 90 | 11.4 | 8.77 | 9.45 |
| 91 | 10.8 | 9.26 | 9.78 |
| 92 | 10.2 | 9.80 | 10.13 |
| 93 | 9.6 | 10.42 | 10.48 |
| 94 | 9.1 | 10.99 | 10.85 |
| 95 | 8.6 | 11.63 | 11.23 |
| 96 | 8.1 | 12.35 | 11.62 |
| 97 | 7.6 | 13.16 | 12.03 |
| 98 | 7.1 | 14.08 | 12.45 |
| 99 | 6.7 | 14.93 | 12.88 |
| 100 | 6.3 | 15.87 | 13.33 |

All ages shown represent the year when you attain the ½ point of the age. An example would be for 70, it would be the actual year you turn 70½. The year you turn 70½ could be different from the year you turn 70, based on whether you turn 70 in the first half or the second half of the year.

**Inflation** is a critical concern when you stop working because you will not be getting pay increases or bonuses to keep up with the devaluation of the dollar. Social Security does give an inflation adjustment, but most pensions do not. If the average inflation rate is 3.5%, $30,000 today will only have the buying power of about $21,300 in 10 years, and in 20 years about $15,100. You will have lost almost half of your buying power within 20 years with a 3.5% inflation rate. This is a significant loss. Consider if inflation took off into the double digits like it did in the '70s and '80s! At a 14% inflation rate, your money's buying power will be cut in half in less than 5 years! This is why everyone should be concerned about the rate of inflation and its adverse effects on your money. The proposed portfolio strategy is set up to minimize the effects of inflation or even take advantage of it. The official inflation number for each year is the consumer price index identified as CPI-U with the U representing the "urban" CPI and can be found on the www.irs.gov or other websites.

**Taxes** on your investments are also a significant variable to consider. It will help your investments if you keep the impact of taxes in mind when you set up your portfolio and make transactions. Most people today approaching or in retirement have their money in tax-deferred accounts, and some people have taxable investments and Roth IRA accounts, also. Money that comes from tax-deferred accounts is taxed as ordinary income. Under certain conditions, withdrawals from Roth accounts are completely tax free. In taxable accounts, withdrawals are taxed based on capital gains.

When after-tax money goes into a Roth account, the earnings are not taxed, if meeting certain qualifications. Taxable accounts have after-tax money going into the account and can be taxed on dividends and capital gains. The taxable account can be taxed every year even when you do not make a withdrawal since dividends/interest and capital gains can occur depending on your investment. If you do make a withdrawal out of a taxable account, you should pay attention to the type of security and the age of the securities sold because short-term capital gains (securities that you have held for twelve months or less) can be taxed as ordinary income whereas long-term capital gains (securities held for more than twelve months) can generally be taxed at a much lower rate. There are types of securities that have tax advantages, such as municipal bonds, when meeting certain conditions, which can avoid federal, state, and local taxes.

# Chapter 8

## Conclusion

This is an excellent strategy for a conservative investment approach before and during retirement. The approach reduces risk by not relying on security growth but instead relies mainly on the cash flow that the selected securities generate. A big advantage for this strategy is that people do not have to lose sleep due to the ups and downs of the market. This strategy allows you to maintain a steady and increasing cash flow while being able to select a time to buy or sell securities, as need be. In the sample portfolio, this strategy showed that from 12/03 to 12/13, $260K was withdrawn while the portfolio value increased from $500K to $845K. Therefore over 10 years, a $500K portfolio generated a total value of $260K + $845K = $1.105M. *Not bad for essentially a passive portfolio!*

www.ingramcontent.com/pod-product-compliance
Ingram Content Group UK Ltd.
Pitfield, Milton Keynes, MK11 3LW, UK
UKHW051008120126
10041UKWH00062B/1720